The World According To

_____

Name

By
C.J. Rilly and Suzette Tyler

Graphic Design by
Brian McVay
Jim Neumann

1724 Vassar Drive
Lansing, MI 48912
517-487-9295
styler@voyager.net
All rights reserved
ISBN 0-9716621-1-8

Printed in Hong Kong

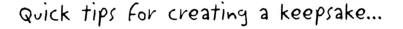

Quick tips for creating a keepsake...

• *Keep a running log of your child's 'gems.'* While most will spill forth spontaneously, you may also want to use the questions throughout the book as 'prompters.' If not, cover those pages up with a photo or tear 'em out. Don't forget to date each entry and just for fun, ask the same question at different ages to see how your child's responses differ.

• *Every child has his/her own vocabulary.* Use the 'dictionary' pages at the end of the book to record those special words and their meanings. From 'pasketti' *(spaghetti)* to 'pic-a-nic-a-nic' *(picnic - he never knows when to stop),* it's great fun.

• *Use a page for family-isms* — expressions used by your family that make no sense to anyone else and originate with a little one's unique interpretation of something, ie. 'dogos' *(hotdogs),* 'squirrel balls' *(walnuts),* 'foot-mommy' *(stepmother).*

ABOUT YOU

What's the best thing about you?

Do you have manners? What are they?

What do you do or wear when you want to look you're very best?

Is there anything you used to be afraid of
but you're not any more?

Is there something you'd really like to do but know you shouldn't?

Tell about a time when you were brave.
...when you were kind.

What will you be when you grow up?

IN YOUR OPINION

What makes someone a good friend?

If you could have anyone in the world as a friend,
who would it be? Why?

What bit of knowledge or piece of advice do you
have that you wish you could pass on to everyone else?

Should children be punished? How?
What about parents?

Is there anything adults are allowed to do that you
think children should be allowed to do also?

What's the prettiest thing you've ever seen?

ON MOM *

*(Use the same questions for Dad, Grandma, Grandpa...
or anyone else.)*

How would you describe your mom to someone
who doesn't know her?

What genes did you get from her?
(How are you alike?)

What's the most fun thing you do with your mom?
How does she make you feel special?

How do you know when your mom is angry?
What makes her angry?

Does she ever act 'silly'?

What's your mom's favorite thing to do?

My mom looks pretty when . . .

Around the house

What's the most important rule in your house?
Who breaks it the most?

Who's the boss in your house? Why?
If you were the boss, what would you make everyone do?

What's the best/worst food that your mom makes?
Tell how she makes it . . . *the recipe.*

What's the best food your dad makes? His worst?

What would you like to eat for breakfast
for the rest of your life?
Lunch? Dinner?

What's the funniest thing you've ever seen around your house?

What's the best secret you know?

ON PARENTS

What's the job of a mom? Of a dad?

What's the most important thing your
mom has taught you?
Your dad?

What do moms and dads do for fun?

What does mom always tell dad?
What does dad always tell mom?

What's the hardest thing about raising children?
Are you hard or easy to raise?

THE SIBLING

What's the best thing about being a
big/little sister/brother?
The worst?

What do you love best about your brother/sister?

What does your brother/sister do that makes you mad?
Have you ever thought of trading him/her in?
For what?

What's the best way to settle an argument?

How many brothers and sisters would you like to have?
What does your mom say?

IMAGINE

Of all the movies you've seen and stories you've read
what person in them would you want to be? Why?

If you were magic,
who or what would you make disappear?

If you could give one thing to everyone in the world
what would it be? Why?

If you could have any pet in the world what would it be?
What trick would you teach it?

If a genie granted you 3 wishes, what would they be?

What would you do if you could be invisible for a day?

If you were to take a spaceship to the moon,
what 3 things from home would you
make sure to bring with you?

MONEY

Are you rich or poor? How do you know?

Who is in charge of money at your house?
What do they do with it?

What does dad do at work all day?
What does mom do at work all day?

If you had all the money in the world,
what would you buy for yourself?
Your mom? Your dad? Your brother/sister?
Grandma/Grandpa? Your friend?

If you had no money, what would you give each of
them?

POLITICS AND RELIGION

If you wrote a letter to the President,
what would you tell him?

If you could make a law that everyone had to obey,
what would it be?

Who is God? What does he/she look like?
What does he/she do?

What do you ask for in your prayers?

What could everyone do to make the world a
nicer place?

LOVE AND MARRIAGE

What is 'love'?

How old should you be to get married?

How do you pick a good husband/wife?
Have you picked anyone?

What will your wedding be like?

How many children and pets will you have?
What will you name them?

Why did your dad pick your mom?
Why did your mom pick your dad?

HOLIDAYS AND YOUR DAY

Have you ever seen Santa Claus? The Easter Bunny?
The Tooth Fairy?

How well do they do their jobs?
(How could they improve?)

What will you be thankful for on Thanksgiving Day?

What's your idea of a 'perfect' birthday party?

If you could be any age, what age would you be?
Why?

How many candles will be on
your mom's/dad's/Grandma's/Grandpa's next cake?

SCHOOL

Who's the smartest person you know?
How can you tell?

What's the most important thing you've
learned at school?

What's the most fun thing to do at your school?
What's not so fun?

If you could change something about your school
or your teacher, what would it be?

What makes your teacher really angry?
Really happy?

Are you 'teacher's pet'? Who is?

My Dictionary